Words to Trade by

notionpress
.com

Words to Trade by

Anirudh Sethi

notionpress
.com

Notion Press

Old No. 38, New No. 6

McNichols Road, Chetpet

Chennai - 600 031

First Published by Notion Press 2015

ISBN: 978-93-52062-26-3

Contents

Discipline

- The ultimate goal is to maximize profitability while minimizing risk. This does not happen by chance. It takes planning, execution and discipline.
- Make no mistake about it, letting a profit run can be a very difficult thing to do psychologically. However, if you are using a longer-term method – which requires at least an occasional "big winner" to offset a lot of small losses, it is imperative to avoid taking profits too soon. Remember the word "discipline".
- A lack of discipline can destroy even the most talented and well-prepared trader.
- Trade a position size that enables you to stay disciplined with entries, exits, and stop losses. Trading too big will lead to errors in judgement.
- Understand yourself, know your time frame, be patient, control impulses, minimize losses, hold winners, b disciplined = consistent success
- Do not worry about losing money that can be made back worry about losing your trading discipline.
- A trader can only go on to success after they have faith in themselves as a trader, their trading system

as a winner, and know that they will stay disciplined in their trading journey.

- A trading plan has to be followed with discipline to have a chance at success.

- A trading plan has to be followed with discipline to have a chance at success.

- Position sizing, discipline, and consistency is the difference in profitable versus unprofitable traders even if they use the same system.

- Trading with small increments of total capital at risk changes everything. Discipline, emotions, stress, and draw downs all become manageable.

- No trading system of robust trading method will be benefit you in the long term if you do not have discipline

- *Don't let the outcome of one trade alter your trading discipline. One trade doesn't make a system...*

- "It is truly amazing how the market will not let traders get away with even a momentary lapse of discipline."

- "Effective money management is not a matter of complexity, but rather a matter of discipline."

- Risk management, Discipline, Willingness to pull the trigger. Apply these to a positive expectancy model and I don't see how you would fail.

- Successful traders have their beliefs about the markets, and have the conviction to trade those beliefs with discipline and good risk control.
- If a market isn't trending, then there's no current opportunity for a trend follower. This is when patience and discipline come to the fore.
- So, what can you control? Your risk per trade, your entry/exit criteria, your patience, discipline and commitment to stick to your rules.
- Have a process with unbreakable discipline. Great trades sometimes come with small losses. Keeping losses in check is key... there is always another day and capital is a trader's lifeblood.
- Discipline trumps conviction.
- No matter how strongly you feel on a given position, you must defer to the principles of discipline when trading. Always attempt to define your risk and never believe that you're smarter than the market.
- Many traders can't (or don't) take the small losses. They often stick with a loser until it really hurts, then take the loss. This is an undisciplined approach...a trader needs to develop and stick with a system.
- Not following a disciplined trading program leads to accepting large losses and small profits. Many traders do not define offensive and defensive plans when an initial position is taken.

- Emotion makes many traders hold a loser too long. Many traders don't discipline themselves to take small losses and big gains.

- Often, traders do not recognize the difference between trading markets and trending markets. Lack of discipline is a major shortcoming.

- Lack of discipline includes several lesser items; i.e., impatience, need for action, etc. Also, many traders are unable to take a loss and do it quickly.

- Many traders have the habit of not cutting losses fast, and getting out of winners too soon. It sounds simple, but it takes discipline to trade correctly. This is hard whether you're losing or winning.

- Futures traders tend to have no discipline, no plan, and no patience. They over trade and can't wait for the right opportunity. Instead, they seem compelled to trade every rumour.

- Lack of self-discipline on the part of the trader and/or broker creates losses. Futures traders tend to do inadequate research.

- Too many traders do not apply money management techniques. They have no discipline, no plan. Many also overstay when the market goes against them, and won't limit their losses

- Be disciplined. Don't feed your ego. In this game capital preservation is key. Live to fight another day. Patience isn't a virtue in trading, it's a necessity...

- Blaming outside forces for poor trading results is an incredibly destructive behaviour. High frequency traders, market makers, and irrational markets, give an undisciplined trader license to make reckless trades. The less responsibility taken for results, the more destructive they can be with an account.

- Trade without discipline and risk management and a trader will be destroyed regardless of their trading system or method.

- Without the right level of discipline you won't follow any trading system long enough to make money no matter how good a system it is.

- *It Is Absolutely Necessary* To Have An Edge You can't win without an edge, even with the world's greatest discipline and money management skills. If you don't have an edge, all that money management and discipline will do for you is to guarantee that you will gradually bleed to death. Incidentally, if you don't know what your edge is, you don't have one.

- Discipline was probably most frequent word used by the exceptional trades that I interviewed. There are two reasons why discipline is critical. Understand *That You Are Responsible*

    - It's a prerequisite for maintaining effective risk control.

    - You need discipline to apply your methods without second guessing and choosing which trade to take.

- A final word, remember that you are never immune to bad trading habits – the best you can do is to keep them latent. As soon as you get lazy or sloppy, they will return!
- A traders discipline and risk management really determine their probability of success more than their trading system.
- Develop an edge, manage risk and have the discipline to keep trading your edge during a draw down and even a genius can succeed in this biz.
- Either you take your trading very seriously and trade your edge with discipline or you become a financial donor to the traders who do.
- The 2 most important Trading attributes? Self-belief and Discipline. Knowing tomorrow that you will make much more than you lost today.
- There is a HUGE difference between chart reading and actually trading for profits. The difference is in position sizing, discipline and flexibility
- Remember that taking losses is part of trading. It's obviously not fun, but it's the most important part of the discipline.
- "The key to trading success is emotional discipline. Making money has nothing to do with intelligence.
- If you have trouble with discipline and commitment, you should avoid trading. It's not for the wishy-washy

- Having trading discipline is the beginning; keeping discipline is the progress; staying discipline is the success.

- Success in trading is directly proportional to discipline and inversely proportional to 'too much' of knowledge

- When you stop judging trades by profit and losses but instead by whether you followed your trading plan with discipline, then you are winning.

- Three areas of strength that all traders need are discipline, patience and confidence. Trading is a marathon not a sprint

- If I could give a gift to my trading friends it would be the gift of discipline and patience. Patience is needed here and for days to come

- Trades made outside a robust system are pointless. Trading an edge with discipline and risk management is how the long term profits are made.

- Trading is not hard, what is hard is self control, discipline, focus, perseverance, and keeping the ego in check.

- Analysing oneself in relation to a trade also improves discipline as anticipation neutralises emotion

- Regrets in your trading should come from your loss of discipline only not a loss of money.

- If u don't have discipline in your trading and your just addicted to the action, make the proper adjustments or else u won't be around long.

- There's a lot of magical thinking regarding trading. Bottom line: This is a business of probabilities and risk management.

- Really profits in trading are made with patience, discipline, and risk management everything else is just details.

- Stock trading is not free money; profit must be earned through homework, discipline, courage, patience, and perseverance in the market.

- In trading, if you are doing the right things with discipline, homework, robust signals, and risk management then time is your greatest ally

- In a tape like today, traders with high levels of conscientiousness shine as they have the self-discipline to remain patient.

- "A trader who has a good chance of success has the following attributes:

  is properly capitalized;
  treats trading like a business;
  has a low tolerance of risk;
  trades only when the market provides an opportunity;
  can control emotions;
  has a trading plan;
  has a risk management plan;

is incredibly disciplined;
is focused; and
has back-tested his trading methodology."

- Have a process w unbreakable discipline. Great trades sometimes come with small losses. Keeping losses in check is key… there is always another day and capital is a trader's lifeblood.

The reality of trading

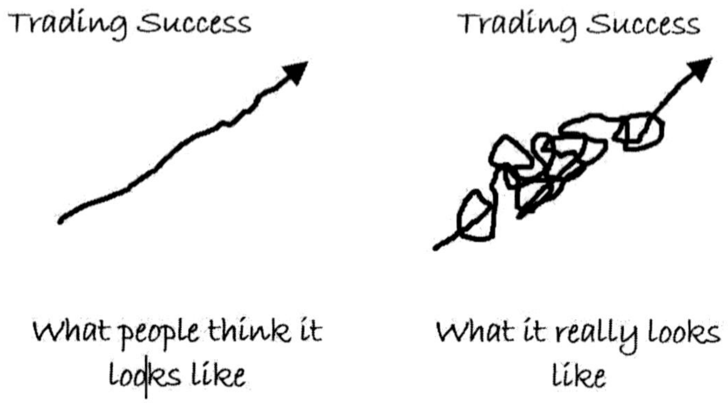

The road to recovery is not linear

% Loss Of Capital	% Of Gain Required To Recover Loss
10%	11.11%
20%	25%
30%	42.85%
40%	66.66%
50%	100%
60%	150.00%
70%	233.00%
80%	400.00%
90%	900.00%
100%	Broke!

Fear

- The costliest mistakes in trading are usually made when the pain of losing money (and/or the fear of losing more money) becomes too great. Bottom line: never risk too much at one time.
- If trading (or any other job or endeavour) is a source of anxiety, fear, frustration, depression, or anger, something is wrong.
- Fear of giving back a small profit will cause a trader to miss the big winning trades.
- The market begins to instil a little fear, but we have yet to learn the first key lesson.
- We are plagued with fear and have no clear methodology.
- But we are still fearful and this remains a big problem. We learnt, some time ago, the necessity of cutting losses; we cannot get to the second secret until we deal with the fear.
- We keep trading and we continue to do OK, we start to get more confident and the fear starts to dissipate.

- We build on our success. Systems improve, results improve, and our mental attitude improves, fear becomes less of a problem.

- We start to move away from fear, and start to become risk-orientated.

- *A poised person is a person who can handle their hopes and their fears in a calm manner.*

- Fear Of Being Stopped Out Or Fear Of Taking A Loss: The usual reason for this is that the trader fears failure and feels like he or she cannot take another loss. The trader's ego is at stake.

- Getting Out Of Trades Too Early: Relieving anxiety by closing a position. Fear of position reversing and then feeling let down. Need for instant gratification.

- Over Thinking The Trade, Second Guessing Your Trading Signals: Fear of loss or being wrong. Wanting a sure thing where sure things don't exist. Not understanding that loss is a part of trading and the outcome of each trade is unknown. Not accepting there is risk in trading. Not accepting the unknown.

- Afraid To Trade: No trading system in place. Not comfortable with risk and the unknown. Fear of total loss. Fear of ridicule. Need for control. Fear of another loss. No trust in your trading.

- Fear Of Being Stopped Out Or Fear Of Taking A Loss: The usual reason for this is that the trader fears failure and feels like he or she cannot take another loss. The trader's ego is at stake.

- Getting Out Of Trades Too Early: Relieving anxiety by closing a position. Fear of position reversing and then feeling let down. Need for instant gratification.

- Over Thinking The Trade, Second Guessing Your Trading Signals: Fear of loss or being wrong. Wanting a sure thing where sure things don't exist. Not understanding that loss is a part of trading and the outcome of each trade is unknown. Not accepting there is risk in trading. Not accepting the unknown.

- Afraid To Trade: No trading system in place. Not comfortable with risk and the unknown. Fear of total loss. Fear of ridicule. Need for control.

- Fear: fearful of profit and one acts too soon.

- People hope when they should fear and fear when they should hope

- Identify your greatest fears and face them as directly as possible, so that you find out they are not as powerful as they seemed.

- Find out what you most fear and then place yourself in a controlled situation where you can directly experience that fear.

- "Trader has to fight two instincts. Instead of hoping he must fear; instead of fearing he must hope."

- "One of the reasons underlying this preoccupation with the fear of losing is that the speculator often over-trades, both in terms of the size of the position as well as the turnover activity of the account. It is essential that the trader control and overcome these urges to over-trade or over position."

- **Fear** – Fear of losing money can make traders skip on a perfectly valid trade. It might also make traders take a small loss on a trade, to then see it turn around and give profit when all the time you were taking the correct steps of entering a stop loss which was never taken out.
- "The larger the trade position, the greater the danger that trading decisions will be driven by fear rather than by judgment and experience"
- Fear is your worst enemy, risk is your best friend!
- There is no more certain recipe for losing than having a fear of losing. If you can't stand taking losses, you will either end up taking large losses or missing great trading opportunities – either flaw is sufficient to sink any chance for success.
- Emotions can affect the trading of our system and methodology. Fear and greed can cause errors in logic and discipline.
- Don't fear losses, not cutting them fast is a crime, managing your loss correctly is one of the aspects in building a robust trading system
- Trading Fear lead into panic and this will result in early trade exits resulting in minimizing your profit
- Decrease your level of fear in order not to miss trading opportunities

- Greed and fear in trading operate under one common element: impatience.
- Fear that your loss will become bigger and always hope that your win will become bigger. That is how to properly use hope and fear
- Regret is not talked about as much as fear and greed, but it's a very powerful emotion in trading
- In trading risk should not be feared it should be managed.
- Most bottoms are made when investors are puking their guts out(fear) and most tops are made when the picture is supremely perfect(greed)

I could say the same for trading indicators

It doesn't matter how many resources you have. If you don't know how to use them, it will never be enough.

This should be your attitude towards trading... If not, you're either gambling or chasing.

GREED

- If you're using your own fear or greed as entry or exit signals you're going to have a bad time trading.
- Buy from the scared, sell to the greedy.
- Emotions can be the enemy of the trader and investor, as fear and greed play an important part of one's decision making process.
- To the best of your ability, try to keep your priorities in-line. Don't let the "greed factor" that Wall Street can generate outweigh other, and just as important, areas of your life. Balance the physical, mental, spiritual, relational, and financial needs of life.
- Fear and greed are stronger than long-term resolve Investors can be their own worst enemy, particularly when emotions take hold. Gains *"make us exuberant; they enhance well-being and promote optimism,"* says Santa Clara University finance professor Meir Statman. His studies of investor behaviour show that *"Losses bring sadness, disgust, fear, regret. Fear increases the sense of risk and some react by shunning stocks."*
- All through time, people have basically acted and reacted the same way in the market as a result of:

greed, fear, ignorance, and hope. That is why the numerical formations and patterns recur on a constant basis.

- Fear, greed, and egos are very expensive things while trading the financial markets.
- Besides sticking to long positions only, the professional always makes trades of even amounts. He isn't like the amateur who lets greed or fear change the size of his trades. The beginner plunges on a trend that suddenly turns, then puts on a light trade on a contrarian situation that does turn around. He keeps switching amounts and positions so that he never has a worthwhile trade on when the market goes his way. He is always one day behind the direction of a stock and several days behind the rhythm of the market.
- Don't get greedy. Remember, bulls and bears make money - pigs get slaughtered.
- As traders, the more we can detach ourselves from the emotions of hope, greed and fear, the better our chances for trading success. Why are there hundreds of good technical analysts but few good traders? Because they need to spend more time on their personal psychology than their analytical methodology.
- Trading Too Much: Need to conquer the market. Greed. Trying to get even with the market for a previous loss. The excitement of trading (similar to Compulsive Trading).

- Irritable after the Trading Day: Emotional roller coaster due to anger, fear, and greed. Putting too much attention on trading results and not enough on the process and learning the skill of trading. Focusing on the money too much. Unrealistic trading expectations.

- Trading With Money You Cannot Afford To Lose Or Trading With Borrowed Money: Last hope at success. Trying to be successful at something. Fear of losing your chance at opportunity. No discipline. Greed. Desperation.

- Not Trading The Correct Position Size: Dreaming the trade will be only profitable. Not fully recognizing the risk and not understanding the importance of money management. Refusing to take responsibility for managing your risk.

- Trading Too Much: Need to conquer the market. Greed. Trying to get even with the market for a previous loss. The excitement of trading (similar to Compulsive Trading).

- Irritable after the Trading Day: Emotional roller coaster due to anger, fear, and greed. Putting too much attention on trading results and not enough on the process and learning the skill of trading. Focusing on the money too much. Unrealistic trading expectations.

- Trading With Money You Cannot Afford To Lose Or Trading

- With Borrowed Money: Last hope at success. Trying to be successful at something. Fear of losing your chance at opportunity. No discipline. Greed. Desperation.

- Too many traders let hope, greed, fear or ignorance lead them to regret. Don't let your emotions determine your trading actions and results.

- Thou shalt not trade with emotion. This includes, fear, greed and lack of discipline. There is no room for it in this equation. Find a way to get a better handle on it, and/or walk away from it. I can tell you from experience that you will have an impossible time being successful at trading when making emotional decisions.

- Impatience, Fear and Greed will make you poor. Any need to trade is rooted in greed and impatience.

- Some traders try to "beat the market" by day trading, nervous scalping, and getting greedy.

- Greed causes some traders to allow profits to dwindle into losses while hoping for larger profits. This is really a lack of discipline. Also, having too many trades on at one time and over-trading for the amount of capital involved can stem from greed.

- Greed, as evidenced by trying to pick tops or bottoms, is a frequent error.

- Greed – You see that your trade is well up and you start picturing that new sports car. You think to yourself "if I could just make 50 % more" but what can often happen in these situations is that your profit disappears and your trade is now under water, all thanks to greed.

- Pain – If you learn to deal with all your emotions such as fear and greed then you will hopefully never experience pain as this one is a tough pill to take. Seeing your hard earned money get swallowed up by the market is financial pain and an emotion we can all do without!

- "Fear, greed, and ego are very expensive monkeys to have on your back while trading.

- When you succumb to fear or greed or ego, you become your own worst enemy. Knowing yourself as well as you do, do you really want you as your worst enemy?

- Losing big money trading is usually caused by: lack of homework, lack of risk management, ego, fear, stubbornness, predictions, or greed

- Nothing destroys more trading accounts than ego, arrogance, & greed mixed with ignorance

- Trading is a mental exercise identifying support and resistance zones. 90% gamble and the other 10% study and understand greed and fear.

- If u are a trader who wants to get rich quit then your greed will redistribute your trading capital to the traders that r getting rich slow

- Emotions can affect the trading of our system & methodology. Fear and greed can cause errors in logic and discipline.

- Traders do not let greed, fear, or ego drag u into doing stupid things with your trading account, self control is just as important as charts
- Your greed wants to chase a trade that has already happened while your trading plan wants to enter a trade before it moves a great deal.
- Trading is primarily a psychological game more than anything. Fear, greed, and pride are a traders kryptonite.
- The best trading method is to take advantage of the crowd's greed and fear. Your trading statement is the receipt, not your spreadsheet.
- The trading is not just about fear and greed, boredom is also very dangerous to successful trading.
- Making trading decisions based solely on ego, fear, or greed is always a mistake whether you win or lose.
- The enemies of good trading are pride, greed, and fear. The friends of good trading are focus, cutting losses quickly, and being humble.
- Profiting from trading is about risk appetite and capital allocation! Conquering fear and greed… Trading is a business… not a gamble!
- Greed and fear in trading operate under one common element: impatience.
- The key to winning at trading is to trade PRICE, not opinions, not beliefs, not hope, not greed, or fear, trade the PRICE ACTION.

- Trading shares is simple maths, two plus three equals five. But our greed makes it seven and our panic reduces it to three

- We get in our own way in trading when we stop trading the chart and begin letting our own fear, greed, and pride make our trading decisions.

- Trading should be like a business, you want to trade off others emotions like greed and fear, not experience them yourself.

- Most bottoms are made when investors are puking their guts out(fear) and most tops are made when the picture is supremely perfect(greed)

- "Trade hungry, not greedy."

The positive circle of trading

This is so true

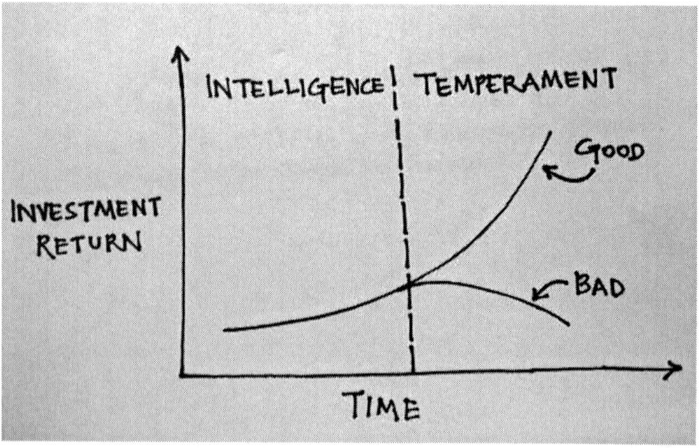

Hope

- The kiss of death is abandoning a stop loss in favour of hope.
- Hope: hope for a change in the forces against one.
- Don't hope the trade will turn back in your favour. If it's not acting right, get out, treat the loss as a cost of doing business and move on.
- **Remember that there is ALWAYS someone on the other side of your trade who is using a trading technique exactly the opposite of yours who hopes to make money with his system.**
- Hope: hope for a change in the forces against one.
- The most reliable pattern of the last few years has been the V-bottom. Many years ago V-bottoms were failure prone, now it has become the best pattern to buy. Here is the scan; the vehicle has to be an ETF (no commodities), look for one that is oversold, down multiple days in a row, buy some, when it accelerates to the downside buy some more, hope the V-bottom pattern continues to work, sell over the next 7 days.
- *Hope is a Four-Letter Word* **Hope is a dirty word for a trader, not only in regards to procrastinating in a losing position, hoping the market will come back, but also in terms of hoping for a reaction that will allow for a better entry in a missed trade.**

If you are making money why do you care?

The trader who does not require validation from anyone is the most Powerful trader on the planet.

Patience

- Patience is the most underrated trait in trading. Better off being patient and missing trades than executing too early.
- Patience is the most underrated trait in trading. Better off being patient and missing trades than executing too early.
- Never trade out of boredom. Trade because the setup is there and price has come to your buy/short point. Write plans, study and have patience.
- Patience is the most underrated trait in trading. Better off being patient and missing trades than executing too early.
- *The other qualification is "***PATIENCE***" to wait for the opportune time, when as many factors as possible are positioned in the traders favour.*
- *Poise and patience are the close friends of successful traders.*
- The market has far more patience than the majority of traders. There is an old saying that the market will do whatever it takes to drive the largest amount of traders crazy. Trends can persist as long as there are traders fighting them. Don't fight the tape.

- It's a marathon, and amazing opportunities come to those with patience, available capital, and a thoughtful plan. Time frames are key and patience can mean waiting an additional 15 minutes, an hour, a day, or a week, or legging into weakness or out of strength similarly. Exiting profitable "long" trades in fractions (while raising stop-loss levels) allows you to let them run and maximizes profits.
- Some speculators don't have the temperament to accept small losses in a trade, or the patience to let winners ride.
- **Exercise patience,** letting a stock's move play out, while paying attention to all the facts – instead of relying on emotions.
- As you may well imagine, some of the quotes attributed to this legendary stock guru remain quite useful today. We can all learn from Mr. Livermore, so here are just a few of his ideas on trading breakout stocks.
- *The Virtue of Patience:* **Waiting for the right opportunity increases the probability of success. You don't always have to be in the market.**
- *The Importance of Sitting:* **Patience is important not only in waiting for right trades, but also in staying with trades that are working. The failure to adequately profit from correct trades is a key profit-limiting factor.**
- **"One common adage… that is completely wrong-headed is: You can't go broke taking profits. That's precisely how many traders *do* go broke.**

While amateurs go broke by taking large losses, professionals go broke by taking small profits."

- Patience isn't a virtue in trading, it's a necessity...
- In trading money flows from those that fight trends to those that follow trends in their time frame over the long term.
- Really profits **in trading** are made with **patience,** discipline, and risk management everything else is just details.
- Right **Trading** Psychology = perseverance, **patience,** focus, faith **in** yourself as a trader and faith **in** your system for performance.
- Learn to develop **patience** and quietness **in** your **trading** – this learned edge will help you trade less and make more.
- Stock **trading** is not free money; profit must be earned through homework, discipline, courage, **patience,** and perseverance **in** the market.
- I have learned through you that the biggest mistake traders make is over-trading - Patience is absolute key and rewarded.
- It's a marathon and amazing opportunities come to those with patience, available capital, and a thoughtful plan. Time frames are key and patience can mean waiting an additional 15 minutes, an hour, a day, or a week, or legging into weakness or out of strength similarly. Exiting profitable "long" trades in fractions (while raising stop-loss levels) allows you to let them run and maximizes profits.

Characteristics of Successful and Unsuccessful Traders

Successful Traders	Unsuccessful Traders
Trades with a plan	Trades impulsively
Trades in a rule-governed fashion	Trades on hunches and urges
Trades when in a clear mental state	Trades emotionally
Trades when focused on the markets	Trades when focused on the self
Becomes problem-focused after a loss	Becomes emotion-focused after a loss
Trades with tested strategies for trade management	Trades with little or no risk management
Trades selectively, based on risk/reward	Trades inconsistently; overtrades and undertrades

Discipline vs. Emotions

Disciplined Traders	Emotional Traders
Trade a defined trading plan.	Trade based on emotions.
Manage risk.	The more confident they are the bigger the trade.
Exit based on predetermined stop.	Exit due to fear.
Enter based on a set up.	Enter based on greed.
Exit a trade when wrong.	Hold a losing trade to prove they are right.
Trade based on price action.	Trade based on their opinions.
Do the homework.	Believe they are special.
Only want to make money.	Want to prove something to some one.
Lose and move on to the next trade.	Blame someone after a losing trade.
Trade with focus and calm.	Trade with stress and strong emotions,
Have a steady state of mind.	Have huge swings in moods.
No one trade means much.	Over celebrate wins and get depressed over losses.

Risk

- Most successful traders focus first on controlling risk, rather than on how much money they plan/ hope to make. In other words, they take care of the losing trades, and the winning trades take care of themselves.
- In the final analysis, proper risk control is ultimately what separates the winning traders from the losing traders.
- Your absolute #1 priority as a trader is to be able to come back and be a trader again tomorrow – never take any risk that might endanger that possibility.
- Trade with a plan so your decisions are made before the markets open, and your emotions put you at risk.
- A trade must have a favourable risk/reward ratio. Your stop loss should be close, while your profit target is farther away.
- A trader has to limit their maximum account drawdown to a level that eliminates their risk of mental ruin. A successful trader stays away from their financial and mental breaking point, and never quits.

- A trader's methodology, plan, and system must match the trader's personality, risk tolerance, and belief system.
- "To make money trading, you have to go against what feels natural as a human. Move TOWARDS risk and away from safety."
- Many traders confuse wanting to make money with looking for a gambling rush. Seek boring, low risk/ volatility set ups and grind out results.
- Many traders confuse wanting to make money with looking for a gambling rush. Seek boring, low risk/ volatility set ups and grind out results.
- Instead of taking a few large positions take many smaller ones. End up having the same potential upside exposure with a fraction of the risk.
- Once in a trade and risk/money management is set don't over think the trade. Direct result will be premature exit. Think less, make more.
- Your risk/reward ratio is: The question of where is the next possible resistance is on the chart versus your initial stop loss.
- On trade entry all we have control over is risk and money management. Dwell on what you can control, NOT on pie in the sky potential profits.
- Once in a trade and risk/money management is set don't over think the trade. Direct result will be premature exit. Think less, make more.

- Most traders' barrier to profitability isn't their method it's their risk management and position sizing.
- In the markets, less = more. Less positions, risk, decisions, hours at the screen and opinions of others = more money
- Understand that the trader only chooses their entries, exits, position size, and risk and the market chooses whether they are profitable or not.
- A trader has to build a trading system that matches their own personality and risk tolerance levels.
- Never risk losing more than 1% of your trading capital on any one trade. Once you lose 1% of your capital you should exit the trade.
- Be very aware of how much risk your total account is exposed to at any one time through position sizing and volatility.
- *Bring your risk of ruin down to almost zero.*

RISK MANAGEMENT

1. Never enter a trade before you know where you will exit if proven wrong.
2. First find the right stop loss level that will show you that you're wrong about a trade then set your positions size based on that price level.

3. Focus like a laser on how much capital can be lost on any trade first before you enter not on how much profit you could make.

4. Structure your trades through position sizing and stop losses so you never lose more than 1% of your trading capital on one losing trade.

5. Never expose your trading account to more than 5% total risk at any one time.

6. Understand the nature of volatility and adjust your position size for the increased risk with volatility spikes.

7. Never, ever, ever, add to a losing trade. Eventually that will destroy your trading account when you eventually fight the wrong trend.

8. All your trades should end in one of four ways: a small win, a big win, a small loss, or break even, but never a big loss. If you can get rid of big losses you have a great chance of eventually trading success.

9. Be incredibly stubborn in your risk management rules don't give up an inch. Defence wins championships in sports and profits in trading.

10. Most of the time trailing stops are more profitable than profit targets. We need the big wins to pay for the losing trades. Trends tend to go farther than anyone anticipates.

- Only take trades that have a skewed risk reward in your favour.
- There's a lot of magical thinking regarding trading. Bottom line: This is a business of probabilities and risk management.
- You don't need luck or **hope in** your **trading** you need math. Probabilities, possibilities, and risk management are what cause success.
- Be advised that the humble and the flexible traders that are the best risk managers end up with all the chips eventually.
- You don't have to increase your risk to increase your return. Those who do will end up broke or quit the profession out of frustration.
- Even the best looking chart can fall apart for no apparent reason. Thus, never fall in love with a position but instead remain vigilant in managing risk and expectations. Use volume as a confirming guidepost.
- Even the best looking chart can fall apart for no apparent reason. Thus, never fall in love with a position but instead remain vigilant in managing risk and expectations. Use volume as a confirming guidepost.
- **If you have money management, you can let volatility go because you know it doesn't have any correlation with risk of ruin. You can use volatility to your advantage.**

- Accept losses to get gains. Risk and reward are always part of the equation.
- Never risk more than 2% of your trading portfolio on any one trade.
- "In-the-money options may sometimes provide a more attractive risk management tool than stops."
- "So what exactly is your methodology?" If you cannot answer that question, you are not ready to be risking money in the markets."
- A successful trader quantifies, analyzes and truly understands and accepts risk. Emotional and psychological acceptance of risk is what determines your mental state in each trade. Individual risk tolerance and preferred trading timeframe make each trader unique. Select a trading methodology that reflects your preferred timeframe and risk tolerance.
- Conservative. They under trade, under trade and under trade. They risk very little of their account on any individual trade. They know how to keep their risk-of-ruin to zero percent.
- Not Trading The Correct Position Size: Dreaming the trade will be only profitable. Not fully recognizing the risk and not understanding the importance of money management. Refusing to take responsibility for managing your risk.
- Accepting the risk in trading

- Trading with money you can afford to risk
- They become euphoric about (and increase risk wildly after) wins.
- They become despondent about (and decrease risk wildly after) losses.
- They set their stop loss based on a 1:1 or 1:2 risk to reward ratio, just to make the ratio look good.
- The answer isn't better analysis, more analysis…the answer is better risk management, better position management.
- Risk managers are not risk averse… risk managers are by definition "managers of risk".
- Establish your risk and stop loss before you hit the buy key.
- Knowing you lose more often than you win helps you risk a low percentage of equity per trade. Low risk and cutting losses quick = small losses.
- Using a trading system is ultimately discretionary. You decide what markets to play, the parameters to buy or sell, how much to risk etc.
- One thing common to all traders, irrespective of how they determine their entries and exits, is good risk control.
- You can open a trade using a system with positive expectancy and good risk control yet still lose. Over the long term though, you will win.

- Successful traders always identify an exit level before entering a new trade. This helps determine their risk per trade.
- Most traders would be better off having simple entry and exit rules, and giving a lot more attention to their risk control and mindset.
- Losses are controlled by proper position sizing and use of stops. Your approach to risk control should also factor in the unexpected.
- Trading too aggressively (e.g. overtrading in poor market conditions, risking too much per trade) can turn a winning system into a losing one.
- Successful traders focus on what they can control (i.e. risk, mindset, following their rules) and let the markets do what they want to do.
- Emotional decisions have a way of coming back to haunt you. If you're personally attached to a position, your decision making process will be flawed. Take a deep breath before risking your hard earned coin.
- Sell hope, buy despair and take the other side of emotional disconnects (in the context of controlled risk). If you can't find the sheep in the herd, chances are that you're it.
- Different investment approaches are warranted at different junctures and applying the right methodology is half the battle. Identify your time horizon and employ a risk profile that allows the market to work for you.

- Maximize your reward relative to your risk.
- If you're patient and pick your spots, edges will emerge that provide an advantageous risk/reward profile. Proactive patience is a virtue.
- Your risk profile should always be an extension of your thought process. If you're unsure, trade smaller until your identify your comfort zone.
- Rationalization has no place in trading. If you put a position on for a catalyst and it passes, take the risk off—win, lose or draw.
- **Asking someone (such as using a service) for advice on where the market is going is a sign you should be on the sidelines until you understand the market better. If the upcoming market direction is not obvious to you, you should not be risking your money. You will lose often enough even when you are right.**
- Many futures traders trade without a plan. They do not define specific risk and profit objectives before trading. Even if they establish a plan, they "second guess" it and don't stick to it, particularly if the trade is a loss. Consequently, they overtrade and use their equity to the limit (are undercapitalized), which puts them in a squeeze and forces them to liquidate positions. Usually, they liquidate the good trades and keep the bad ones.
- They fail to pre-define risk, add to a losing position, and fail to use stops.

- Taking too big a risk with too little profit potential is a sure road to losses.
- Lack of risk capital in the market means inadequate capital for diversification and staying power in the market.
- Traders don't clearly identify and then adhere to risk parameters; i.e., stops.
- "If you don't respect risk, you will be poor."
- Remember, big losses can begin with small losses.
- While it is always possible that the stock will rebound, causing you to sell a good investment, you can help mitigate losses during a bear market with carefully placed stop orders. You are managing your risk. And you will live to invest another day.
- No matter which way you think the market is heading, if you own stocks you must know what has to happen to cause you to sell. Sometimes it is a change in the fundamentals, and other times the market reacts in advance to tell you something is wrong. That will be the time to consider managing risk rather than seeking that last nickel of profit.
- "Risk control is essential, as large percentage losses require increasingly greater percentage gains to get back to even."
- "Trade confidence is relevant not only in determining the trade size, but also in deciding on the right risk management."

- Only risk 1% of your total capital on any one trade idea with position sizing and stop losses, this will determine whether you make it or not in the long term.
- To make more money, risk less.
- Add risk when you are winning, reduce risk when you are losing.
- Difference between great traders and the rest isn't magic entry points, instead they're better risk managers and better at position management.
- Your stop loss versus your upside potential target = risk/reward <— every time you make a trade, do this calculation
- **Trading with no plan and making decisions based on feelings, is a really bad idea. Letting opinions and predictions be a guide to entries, and emotions be a guide to exits, guarantees maximum destruction of trading capital.**
- **Trade first and learn how to trade later. Traders who don't spend time educating themselves before trading will learn the hard way, and give their trading capital to other traders as tuition.**
- **Focusing on ego and the desire to be right, instead of profitability and big losses, will quickly destroy a trader's account.**
- **Traders that fight the trend and disagree with the actual price action will give their trading capital to those that follow the trend.**

- **If a trader doesn't diversify their life with strong relationships, fun, peace, and health, their trading results become too entangled with their self worth. This can lead to mental and emotional ruin.**

- Without the right risk management you will eventually give back all your profits regardless of how good your trading system is.

- Small losses are a cost of doing business. Big losses are usually a result of traders losing control of their emotions, or risking too much.

- **Money Management and Risk Control Money management is even more important than the trading method. The Trading Plan**

  - Never risk more than 5% of your capital on any trade.

  - Predetermine your exit point before you get in a trade.

  - If you lose a certain predetermined amount of your starting capital (say 10 to 20%), take a breather, analyze what went wrong, and wait till you feel confident and have a high-probability idea before you begin trading again.

- *Developing a Low-Risk Idea* **The merit of a low risk idea is that it combines two essential elements: patience (because only a small portion of ideas will qualify) and risk control (inherent in the definition). "Open a doughnut shop next door to a police station".**

- *You Can't Win If You Have To Win* **"Scared money never wins". If you are risking money you can't afford to lose, all the emotional pitfalls of trading will be magnified. The market seldom tolerates the carelessness associated with traders born of desperation.**
- Without the right **risk** management you will eventually give back all your profits regardless of how good your **trading** system is
- Difference between great traders and the rest isn't magic entry points, instead they're better risk managers and better at position management.
- If anyone argues with the 1% of capital at **risk** per trade rule then they probably don't understand the **risk** of ruin.
- "If you don't respect **risk**, you will be poor."
- There's a lot of magical thinking regarding trading. Bottom line: This is a business of probabilities and risk management.
- Difference between great traders and the rest isn't magic entry points, instead they're better risk managers and better at position management.
- Really profits **in trading** are made with **patience**, discipline, and risk management everything else is just details.
- The longer I trade the more I am convinced that position sizing and **risk** exposure will determine your **trading** success **in** the long term.

- Zero **risk** management **in trading** eventually ends badly. The only question is when.
- Entries and exits, emotional management, and **risk** management tend to be much harder **in** real **trading** than just writing a newsletter.
- **In Trading** Accuracy is not as important as Reward to **Risk** Ratio.
- If there is a Holy Grail of **trading** it is **in** the math. **Risk**/Reward, **risk** management, **risk** of ruin, probabilities, and position sizing matters most.
- **Trading** a swing off an oscillator indicator is not the same and “calling” a top or bottom. It is **trading** with a **risk**/reward **in** your favour.
- Eliminating the **risk** of ruin **in** one easy step. If you only **risk** 1% of your **trading** capital on every trade your odds of ruin or almost 0%.
- The most robust **trading** system **in** the world is completely useless **in** the long term without the proper management of the **risk** of ruin.
- If you don’t manage your **risk in trading** then your method really doesn’t even matter because you will end up back lower than you started.
- If you understand and accept **risk** of ruin, you will never **risk** too much again **in** your **trading**.

- Trading is math (specifically statistics), not magic... develop a positive expectancy model, manage the risk and you will succeed.

- Never mirror another trader since you have no idea when style drift occurs, how they handle a black swan event, when they break risk mgmt.

Drawdowns based on percent of account at risk & consecutive losses.

Consecutive losing trades	%-risk per single trade 1%	2%	4%	5%	6%	7%
2	1.99%	3.96%	7.84%	9.75%	11.64%	13.51%
3	2.97%	5.88%	11.53%	14.26%	16.94%	19.56%
4	3.94%	7.76%	15.07%	18.55%	21.93%	25.19%
5	4.90%	9.61%	18.46%	22.62%	26.61%	30.43%
6	5.85%	11.42%	21.72%	26.49%	31.01%	35.30%
7	6.79%	13.19%	24.86%	30.17%	35.15%	39.83%
8	7.73%	14.92%	27.86%	33.66%	39.04%	44.04%
9	8.65%	16.63%	30.75%	36.98%	42.70%	47.96%
10	9.56%	18.29%	33.52%	40.13%	46.14%	51.60%

Probability of a losing streak based on winning percentage

	Probability of X successive losing trades within a 50 trade period									
Win rate	2	3	4	5	6	7	8	9	10	11
5%	100%	100%	100%	100%	100%	100%	100%	100%	100%	100%
10%	100%	100%	100%	100%	100%	100%	100%	100%	100%	100%
15%	100%	100%	100%	100%	100%	100%	100%	100%	100%	100%
20%	100%	100%	100%	100%	100%	100%	100%	100%	99%	97%
25%	100%	100%	100%	100%	100%	100%	99%	96%	91%	82%
30%	100%	100%	100%	100%	100%	98%	92%	82%	69%	55%
35%	100%	100%	100%	100%	97%	89%	75%	59%	43%	30%
40%	100%	100%	100%	98%	88%	71%	52%	35%	22%	14%
45%	100%	100%	99%	91%	72%	49%	30%	18%	10%	5%
50%	100%	100%	95%	77%	51%	29%	16%	8%	4%	2%
55%	100%	99%	86%	58%	31%	15%	7%	3%	1%	1%
60%	100%	96%	70%	38%	17%	7%	3%	1%	0%	0%
65%	100%	88%	51%	22%	8%	3%	1%	0%	0%	0%
70%	99%	73%	32%	11%	3%	1%	0%	0%	0%	0%
75%	96%	53%	17%	4%	1%	0%	0%	0%	0%	0%
80%	87%	32%	7%	2%	0%	0%	0%	0%	0%	0%
85%	67%	15%	2%	0%	0%	0%	0%	0%	0%	0%
90%	39%	5%	1%	0%	0%	0%	0%	0%	0%	0%
95%	12%	1%	0%	0%	0%	0%	0%	0%	0%	0%

STRATEGY

- Instead of adapting to changing markets, remain patient, stick to a proven strategy/style and wait for the markets to fit your criteria
- If your trading strategy doesn't have an edge then you're the punter and the markets are the casino.
- If you are not sure and don't have an edge, cash IS a strategy.
- Pick one strategy and stick to it. This may take time if you are a beginner.
- "If you don't have an edge then the optimal money mgmt strategy is to bet it all at once–the epitome of bad money mgmt."
- Hope is not a viable strategy for trading or investing in anything.
- Stay really strong in body, mind and spirit because you never know when the tsunami is going to hit.
- Focus on execution (trade the right strategy for the idea)

- Knowing when to exit a winning trade, as well as knowing when to exit a losing trade, should be an important part of your overall strategy.
- *"While a consistent, viable strategy is part is clearly the main-stay of successful speculation, three additional traits are required: discipline, discipline and discipline."*
- **Learn to trade before you trade. If you win or lose without understanding why, you will never develop a winning strategy.**
- People that don't believe **in trading** don't understand that outliers all manage the **risk** of ruin, trade a tested strategy and are disciplined.
- Always change a losing game; never change a winning game.
- Always have a plan going into a match, and a backup plan.
- Always have a surprise to pull out all the stops.
- Reconnoitre your opponent before the match for his strengths and weaknesses.
- Have a general strategy against all power players, and another against all control players.
- Analyze every match – how would you play it differently next time.
- Keep a log of your strategies, and of the opponents.

- Always have a customized strategy against each opponent, if possible.
- Call a timeout whenever you skip two straight shots, or the opponent runs three straight points.
- Keep a coach in the crowd for a second opinion.
- Have an offensive second serve, such as the jam or Z.
- Save your upset serve, for example a crack ace, for game winning points.
- Have a no-fail strategy that kicks in in the worst case scenario.
- Define your strengths and weaknesses between tournaments, and drill the latter.
- Set a goal, and time increments to achieve it.
- Resist the norm – The way to the top is almost always a way no one else has tried.
- Don't share your personal original strategies during your competitive career.
- Find one edge against an opponent, or the field, and repeat it over and over.
- Make your backhand as strong as your forehand.
- Know the counters to all your strategies.
- If an opponent throws something at you during a match that you can't handle, hit the same at him next point to know how to respond.

- Use a slow game pace against a rabbit, and a fast pace against a sloth.
- Always volley the ball when possible.
- Always take the most aggressive shot possible during a rally.
- Be able to hit five perfect consecutive ceiling balls as a fallback.
- Match your physical attributes with your strategies, for example condition, age, grace. Elephant tusks cannot grow out of a dog's mouth.
- Pick an overall strategy that is fun to play.
- Strategy evolves on the sweaty hardwood, not in ivory towers, so think as you play practice matches.
- Agree with your practice partner to pause after each game to dissect each other's play.
- Ask every instructor or pro you meet for his best secret strategy.
- Ask better players to critique your strategies.
- The best place to glean strategic titbits is by watching good players, or at a pro stop.
- Unclutter the Clutter. Stop the mechanism. Have a sure-fire mantra or method to calm down instantly.
- Develop a 'Muehleisen's Rheostat' at will of being able to crank up or down your intensity of play by 10%.

- Fight first and save thoughts of victory for later.
- The highest form of generalship is to conquer the gamesman by a stratagem.
- At the beginner level a defensive strategy wins, but at an advanced level the most offensive strategy always wins.
- Have one strategy for a slow ball and another for a fast ball.
- The best general strategy is to serve and shoot.
- Go to the ceiling if the rival runs a string of points.
- Go for the jugular with aces and cracks when you have momentum.
- The shot to practice the most is the kill, because it's the only stepping stone.
- The serve to practice the most is the drive, as it's the most forceful in an aggressive game.
- Save your best strategy for the ripest time - pick the flower when it is ready to be picked.
- When you go up to the mountain often, you will eventually encounter the tiger, so be ready.
- During a reconnoitre find a tiny edge. A tiny is the best soldier that quickly becomes an army.
- Strategy is about setting yourself apart from the competition: it's a matter of being different at what you do.

- Always have a backup service strategy.
- The greatest tactic is to be able to execute at the worst times.
- To win by strategy is no less the role of a general.
- Practice the weakest link in the chain of each of your last performances.
- Have a short term goal and a long term goal at all times.
- Use glass to your advantage with serves and shot selection.
- Shot selection is the most common trait of a win, and flaw of a loss.
- Have pre-designed strategies for every game style.
- The greatest strategy is to commit no mental or physical errors in a match.
- If you're losing a match, is it because your strategy is failing or because of faulty execution of strategy?
- Use a new strategy a hundred times in practice before taking it to a tournament.
- When in doubt grab the bull by the horns.
- Nothing is more beautiful in sport than a well-conceived plan that's executed flawlessly against a superior opponent for a win.

Study strategy over the years to achieve the spirit of the warrior.

Break the cycle

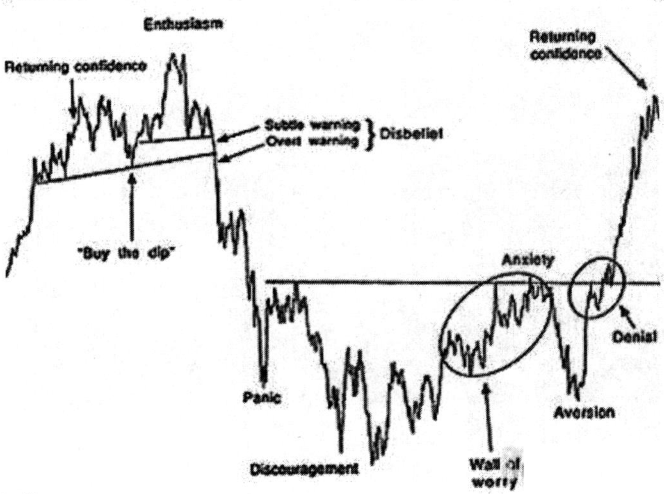

Trading in the sweet spot

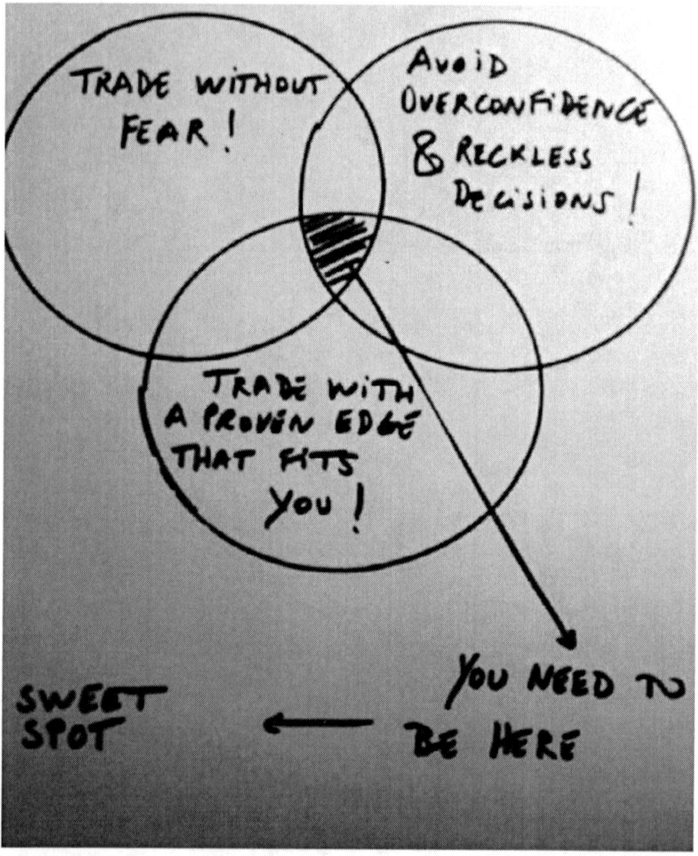

Trading Mantras

Too many traders enter the markets without the slightest realistic idea as to how they will succeed in the long run. Does that sound like a plan for success?

It is essential to trade in a manner that fits your own personality.

There is no "one best way" to trade.

The question that needs to be answered is simply what approach works best for you.

Some traders operate best using a very short-term timeframe. Others operate best using a very long-time timeframe. It is critical to understand your own preference. If you can't bring yourself to hold a trade for more than a few days, it does you no good to use a longer-term trading approach. Likewise, if you have developed a successful longer-term approach and/or don't have time to watch a quote screen, it is a mistake to try to day trade.

If you develop some set criteria for entering trades, and if you have some realistic reason to expect this criteria to generate good returns over time, and you follow that criteria consistently, you give yourself the best chance for success.

Your answer to the question "what criteria will I use to exit a trade at a loss" may have more of an impact on your ultimate success or failure as a trader than any other single factor.

The truest thing to know about trading is that there will be losing trades, and that you must be prepared to deal with them, both financially and psychologically.

The key to long term trading success is to select some method that you will use when you have money on the line and then to stick to it once you are actually trading.

Whenever you hear a successful trader say "what you need to do in order to succeed is…" what they should be saying is "what I need to do in order to succeed is…" What you need to do in order to succeed may be different. Likewise it is your responsibility to determine which ideas from other traders are useful to you and which are not (Warning: it's not always an easy process).

Forming a comprehensive trading plan is your first step toward trading success.

Successful traders learn that the ability to identify the current trend is far more useful than a thousand predictions.

The goal in trading is to make money of course. However, one trade-off that needs to be considered is the relationship between total profitability and the volatility experienced along the way. If the day-to-day volatility is too great, this will often result in a trader "pulling the plug" at exactly the wrong time.

If you "bet the ranch." prepare to have your trading account "buy the farm."

The most cruel paradox in trading is that short-term success can sow the seeds for long-term failure. Beware the trader who has unexpected success and then believes he or she has developed "the touch."

If you decide that you will exit a particular trade if and when a certain set of criteria is met, then that is exactly what you need to do. The specific chain of events that cause your exit criteria to be met are completely irrelevant.

The markets do not know that you or long or short and do not move in a particular way simply to inflict pain upon you personally. It just seems that way sometimes.

The markets will frustrate you and inflict pain upon you from time to time. This is simply a fact of trading life. The real trick is to not inflict pain upon yourself.

Too many traders spend too much time saying things like "I should have gotten in sooner," or "I should have held on longer," "I can't believe that stock reversed the minute I got out," etc., etc., etc. The cure for this is to focus solely on the action of the market from the time you enter the trade until the time you exit the trade. What happened before you got in and after you got out is not important.

Another paradox: it is important to analyze your approach from time to time to see what's working and what's not. However, the danger is that if you are constantly tinkering with your existing approach, you may never truly develop the confidence you need to have in it in order to stick with it when the going gets tough.

In the long run, it is not any prediction you might make about what will happen next that will make the biggest difference in your success or failure, but rather how you react when things don't go the way you expect them to.

Second-guessing a trading decision is the single most simple act in all of trading.

Likewise, watching a trade continue to pile on profits after you have exited prematurely is one of the most painful experiences in all of trading.

In the end, you – and you alone – are ultimately responsible for your own trading success or failure. Remind yourself of this from time to time.

Working past a really bad trading experience can be very difficult. The key is to understand and accept the simple fact that this is part of life as a trader and to not allow a bad experience to have a negative residual effect on your subsequent trades.

The great paradox of option buying:

Lesson A) to maximize your return on any single trade, buy an inexpensive out-of-the-money option.

Lesson B) to maximize your return in the long rung avoid lesson A.

To put it another way, to make money in the long run, avoid trying to make all the money in the world in the short run.

In choosing which option to buy an option buyer must decide which is more important to him or herself – greater upside potential (out-of-the-money) or a higher probability of profit (further in – the-money). There is no exact right or wrong answer. The problem is that too many traders never ask the question. They simply go for the greatest leverage.

In the long run, due to the negative effect of time decay, option buyers generally are better off reducing their leverage and buying options with some intrinsic value, rather than just buying cheap out-of-the-money options.

The questions you need answers for:

- What is my reason for entering this trade?
- What is my objective in entering this trade?
- What is my maximum profit potential and what is the probability of achieving it?
- What is my maximum risk and what is the probability of achieving that?
- Will I need to adjust this position?
- If so, at what point do I need to adjust and what type of adjustment will likely be required?

Am I going to be able to keep track of this trade closely enough to avoid any potential disasters?

If you don't have answers for these questions before entering a particular trade, this should be your warning not to take the trade in the first place.

- Irrational exuberance drives markets way beyond what's "rational". Don't trade based on what's sane, but anticipate the herd's reaction.
- "When you first start trading, forget about TRYING to make money. Focus on the process of learning and execution, and the money will come!"

Don't be a hero

Don't be a hero.

Don't have an ego.

Always question yourself and your ability.

Don't ever feel that you are very good. The second you do, you are dead.

- Trading isn't predicting the future; it's a game of probabilities.
- If you're method has an edge, your P&L is simply an expression of how well you control your actions
- Never short a dull market or waste all day watching it either.
- To be a profitable trader you will need either a high probability winning system or really big winning trades to offset the small losers
- Good fundamentals will show you WHAT to buy good. Options activity will show WHO is buying. good technical research will show WHEN to buy
- Hardest part in trading is how to "keep things simple"
- That is one aspect of teaching that is common in trading. Many won't listen until after they have been decimated. Learn from others mistakes
- A trading method allows one to ride though chop and maintain accounts while waiting for the next big winner to form. Stalk – Strike – Repeat
- A painful market for those traders not being selective with entries. This is something a trader can fix with rules like requiring a base.

Advanced traders tend to do the opposite of beginners.

- Buy their pain, not their gain.
- Successful traders are quick to change their minds and have little pride of opinion.
- ***"The market is a collision of random events, spiced with human emotions and fundamental realities."***
- Every trader should analyze their **trading** after each day to learn from **mistakes** and improve their skills.
- "Opinions don't matter. Positions speak for themselves."
- Trade your plan, your rules, your style, your time frame. Never trade an opinion or someone else's plan. Remember it is your wallet.
- It is usually most profitable to trade in the direction of least resistance for your time frame and trading vehicle.
- If you want to be a great trader, be a sponge soaking up all things stock market. Define your style and keep your system simple.
- A trading plan does not guarantee you will be profitable on each trade. It gives you a road map to calm emotions and show probability of success

- "Self sabotage is when you repeat the same **mistakes** over and over again."
- Technical analysis is a windsock, not a crystal ball. It is a skill that improves with experience and study. Always be a student, there is always someone smarter than you!
- "Thou Shall Not Trade Against the Trend."
- Let volatility work in your favour, not against you.
- Watch what our "Politicos" do, not say.
- Markets tend to regress to the mean over time.
- Portfolios heavy with underperforming stocks rarely outperform the stock market!
- When trading, if a stock doesn't perform as expected within a short time period, either close it out or tighten your stop-loss point.
- As long as a stock is acting right and the market is "in-gear," don't be in a hurry to take a profit on the whole position, scale out instead.
- Never let a profitable trade turn into a loss and never let an initial trading position turn into a long-term one because it is at a loss.
- It's not the stocks that you sell that go higher that matters, it's the stocks you don't sell which go lower, that do.

- Don't think you can consistently buy at the bottom nor sell at the top. This can rarely be consistently done.
- Don't buy a stock simply because it has had a big decline from its high and is now a "better value;" wait for the market to recognize "value" first.
- Don't average trading losses, meaning don't put "good money" after "bad."
- Your odds of success improve when you buy stocks when the technical pattern confirms the fundamental opinion.
- We can't control the stock market. The very best we can do is to try to understand what the stock market is trying to tell us. As I like to say, "Overweight Statistical Probability. Underweight Emotion!"
- Understanding mass psychology is just as important as understanding fundamentals and economics.
- When investing, remain objective. Don't have a preconceived idea or prejudice. Said another way, "the great names in our business … the Paul Tudor Joneses; the Steve Cohens; the Andy Halls; the George Soros'…all have this same trait: the ability to shift on a dime when the shifting time comes."

- Any dead fish can go with the flow. Yet it takes a strong fish to swim against the flow. In other words, what seems "hard" at the time is usually, over time, right.
- Don't make investment or trading decisions based on tips. Tips are something you leave for good service.
- Where there is smoke, there is fire – bad news is usually not a one-time event, more usually follows.
- We are intrigued by the market and start to do some preliminary reading and research.
- We buy a book or two and perhaps some newsletters.
- We find something we quite like and start doing some research using this particular technique.
- We dabble a bit in the market. Trading every now and then, mainly losing money, but not much, and having the occasional winner.
- We generally forget about the losers and congratulate ourselves on our winners. Convincing ourselves that once we learn the techniques better there will be fewer of the former and more, lots more, of the latter.
- We keep manual charts, which may become quite large physically, and maybe plot a few indicators manually (this was before computers became quite so available).

- We spot an approach to the market we think cannot fail to win!
- We start to trade actively.
- The results make it clear that it is not as easy as appeared to be the case. There were a few key points we failed to fully appreciate.
- We continue to trade. Results are fairly indifferent (to bad) but there are enough profits to keep the interest up.
- We continue to expect great results.
- Trading volume increases and the amount of money in the market grows.
- We continue to read and take newsletters, but our research has only scratched the surface. We still have no real idea what we are involved with.
- Our technique scores a major success (the 1987 crash), but our lack of trading skills means that we do not profit from it as we might.
- We keep trading in size. We are overtrading and clearly act as a fugitive from the law of averages. It is only a matter of time.
- We make a big profit. It is all going well, we start to get overconfident.
- We suffer a big loss. Psychological problems start to develop.
- We start to monitor many more indicators.

- We look at other techniques and other markets.
- We get wiped out.
- It becomes clear this is not at all as easy as it looks.
- We become impossible to live with.
- It also becomes clear that the information we used is not much use to those seeking to make money from trading.
- We determine to fill this void and look to create a newsletter telling it how it is.
- We work with an analyst in the USA. Note how inappropriate this is for someone who wants to trade. Much better to work with a trader.
- We continue to trade, but in a much reduced manner.
- We start our newsletter which is an immediate success.
- This requires a lot of research plus a lot of analysis, but it is still not clear that trading is a psychological issue and that the externals (systems/software/computers/brokers/advisers, etc.) are almost completely irrelevant until the internal set up is right.
- It becomes clear that judgmental trading (without a clear methodology) is a dead end.
- We start to look for a suitable methodology.

- Those available on the market do not seem to be suitable and so we design our own.
- We start to trade using a clear methodology. This is not easy but some things start to become obvious.
- We find ourselves trading for no good reason (something that was impossible to detect before we had a clear methodology), but then realize that it is due to an argument earlier. Self esteem clearly plays a role.
- We realize that the key element in trading is our own mentality. Now we can start to make some real progress
- We improve our systems and start to make some money on a one contract basis.
- We take another big hit.
- We feel awful and we think we should perhaps give up, should perhaps have given up some years ago when it all went wrong the first time.
- We keep trading and determine not to get overconfident again. We reinforce the stress management systems we had to learn in the early days and keep meditating (essential to trading success). We realize the importance of remaining humble and also of being an "empty vessel". If you are full of yourself there is no room of learning anything else.

- We meet another trader who becomes a mentor. He introduces a new technique to us, which immediately "fits". This is because we now have the right attitude.
- We decide to see a trading coach/psychologist and have an initial meeting.
- We make a big profit by letting profits run. We have managed to do what every successful trader must. Can we repeat this trick?
- We realize that mental attitude is all. We see that it is vital to be relaxed, we reduce position size, again!
- We spend a few days in the USA working in a group with our trading coach psychologist.
- We begin to make money with consistency.
- We get a little overconfident again! But this time we realise the fact and the damage is limited.
- We start to trade almost subconsciously some of the time. We are becoming expert.
- We know there are still many challenges ahead, but we are confident that we will deal with them.
- Money ceases to be a problem, we truly live in a world of abundance.
- We find that our lives improve across the board and that we are achieving in wide range of areas.

Skill + Strategy = Trading Success

Commandment #1: "Thou Shall Not Trade Against the Trend."

- Portfolios heavy with underperforming stocks rarely outperform the stock market!
- There is nothing new on Wall Street. There can't be because speculation is as old as the hills. Whatever happens in the stock market today has happened before and will happen again, mostly due to human nature.
- Sell when you can, not when you have to.
- Bulls make money, bears make money, and "pigs" get slaughtered.
- We can't control the stock market. The very best we can do is to try to understand what the stock market is trying to tell us.
- Understanding mass psychology is just as important as understanding fundamentals and economics.
- Learn to take losses quickly, don't expect to be right all the time, and learn from your mistakes.
- Don't think you can consistently buy at the bottom or sell at the top. This can rarely be consistently done.
- When trading, remain objective. Don't have a preconceived idea or prejudice. Said another way, "the great names in Trading all have the same trait: An ability to shift on a dime when the shifting time comes."

- Any dead fish can go with the flow. Yet, it takes a strong fish to swim against the flow. In other words, what seems "hard" at the time is usually, over time, right.
- When trading, if a stock doesn't perform as expected within a short time period, either close it out or tighten your stop-loss point.
- As long as a stock is acting right and the market is "in-gear," don't be in a hurry to take a profit on the whole positions. Scale out instead.
- Never let a profitable trade turn into a loss, and never let an initial trading position turn into a long-term one because it is at a loss.
- Don't buy a stock simply because it has had a big decline from its high and is now a "better value;" wait for the market to recognize "value" first.
- Don't average trading losses, meaning don't put "good" money after "bad." Adding to a losing position will lead to ruin. Ask the Nobel Laureates of Long-Term Capital Management.
- Human emotion is a big enemy of the average investor and trader. Be patient and unemotional. There are periods where traders don't need to trade.
- Wishful thinking can be detrimental to your financial wealth.

- Don't make investment or trading decisions based on tips. Tips are something you leave for good service.
- Where there is smoke, there is fire, or there is never just one cockroach: In other words, bad news is usually not a one-time event, more usually follows.
- Realize that a loss in the stock market is part of the investment process. The key is not letting it turn into a big one as this could devastate a portfolio.
- Said another way, "*It's not the ones that you sell that keep going up that matter. It's the one that you don't sell that keeps going down that does.*"

"Let the trade come to you; don't think you're going to force conditions in the market that aren't there."

The more arrogant and ego driven a trader is the higher the probability that they blow up their whole account at any level pro or rookie.

One key to being a profitable trader is to consistently not do anything stupid. Long term this matters a lot. Stupid decisions are expensive

Profitable traders have trading systems. Unprofitable traders trade based on opinions and emotions which are terrible signals.

A winning trade outside a quantified process has little meaning. A losing trade inside a winning system also has little meaning.

"Trading is a matter of probabilities. Even the best trading processes will lose a significant percentage of the time."

"A losing trade that adheres to a profitable strategy is still a good trade b/c if similar trades repeated process will win on balance."

"Do not confuse concepts of winning and losing trades with good and bad trades. Good trade can lose money and bad trade can make…"

"To win at trading, you need to understand that losing is part of the game."

"Amateur traders lose money because they try to avoid losing. Professional traders understand they need to take losses to win."

"If you get out even, you can say, "I was not wrong. I didn't make a mistake." That need not to be wrong is exactly why people lose"…

"I was able to become a winning trader when I was able to say, "to hell with my ego, making money is more important."

"The idea that #trading success is tied to finding some specific ideal approach is misguided. There is no single correct methodology"

"Were it not for their relentless persistence, many of the Market Wizards would never have discovered their ultimate potential."

"In trading, just as in archery, whenever there is effort, force, straining, struggling, or trying, it is wrong."

"You have to learn to let the arrow shoot itself"

"If you are out of sync with the markets, trying harder is often likely to make matters even worse."

"If trading is going well, it will seem effortless. if trading is not going well, you can't force it right by working harder."

"The hard work in trading comes in the preparation. The actual process of trading, however, should be effortless."

"It is a quirk of trading that you could be successful for the short-term without knowing anything; that possibility fools people"

"The possibility of short-term trading success by pure luck beguiles people into thinking trading is a lot easier than it is."

"Trading is probably the world's only profession in which a rank amateur has a 50–50 chance of being right in the beginning."

"But the fact is that the people who are really successful in trading are tremendously hard workers. Why are so many people attracted to trading? Because it seems like an easy way to make a lot of money."

The key attributes of a successful trader are being open-minded and critically challenging general trading knowledge

Cutting losing trades when price comes back to your entry is one of the biggest mistakes you can make. Don't trade based on emotions.

If you miss trades or flip through charts like a lunatic, get the ultimate trading plan!

Process v Outcome

	Good Outcome	Bad Outcome
Good Process	**Deserved Success**	**Bad Break**
Bad Process	**Dumb Luck**	**Poetic Justice**

New Trader vs. Rich Trader Thinking

Difference In Thinking

Beginner
Fears = Cut Winners
Hope = Keep Losers

Professional
Fear = Cut Losers
Hope= Keep Winners

In trading, money is like soap, the more you play with it the smaller it gets."

Three steps to self improvement as a trader: 1) What is the problem? 2) Why do I have this problem? 3) What am I doing to solve it?

The market is designed to take your money. Unexpected moves are designed to shake your confidence and react with an emotional response

Conviction is the by-product of deep learning and experience in the markets. Without conviction it's difficult to achieve consistent returns.

A good trader can make money in any environment as long as he reacts and doesn't anticipate.

Successful traders are mentally agile, adaptive and continually striving for improvement. They embrace uncertainty and LOVE the game.

When you win, say nothing. When you lose, say less. When you start patting yourself on the back for being smarter than markets, start selling!

3 questions to check if you are serious about trading: (1) Do I have a journal? (2) Do I have a trading plan (3) Do I analyze past trades

"Always wait for the setup: No Setup-No Trade."

Speculators are willing losers who often win; gamblers are willing winners who often lose.

It's not the market that defines whether a participant is a Gambler or a Speculator, it's his behaviour.

Profitability - 5 Points

1. Commit to doing the work required to be a successful trader.

2. Create a trading system that captures trends in your time frame. A trader has to be on the right side of the trend in their time frame. The path of least resistance is where you will find the best odds of profitability.

3. Your entries should put the probabilities of profits on your side. Back testing, pattern recognition, and chart studies will give you an edge over those that trade based on opinions.

4. A trader can only be profitable with either a high winning percentage or big wins and small losses. Combining the two is the path to profitable trading.

5. Your system should ensure that you will have the right position when huge moves take place.

TRADER PSYCHOLOGY

1. Be flexible and go with the flow of the markets price action, stubbornness, egos, and emotions are the worst indicators for entries and exits.

2. You must have a trading plan before you start to trade, that has to be your anchor in decision making.

3. You have to let go of wanting to always be right about your trade and exchange it for wanting to make money. The first step of making money is to cut a loser short the moment it is confirmed that you are wrong.

4. Never trade position sizes so big that your emotions take over from your trading plan.

5. "If it feels good, don't do it." – Richard Weissman

6. Trade your biggest position sizes during winning streaks and your smallest position sizes during losing streaks. Not too big and trade your smallest when in a losing streak.

7. You have to have passion for learning to trade; passion is the energy that you need to take you to your goals.

8. You have to have the perseverance to keep going after you want to give up. 90% of new traders quit when they were very frustrated while 100% of successful traders didn't quit until they reached their goals

9. New traders spend too much time looking for what to trade instead of focusing on who they are as traders. You have to know who you are as trader first then you can start building your trading system.

10. Traders have to be able to manage their stress by trading inside their current comfort zone. Traders have to grow themselves and trade size step by step.

11. The vast majority of new traders fail simply because they did not do their homework before they started trading.

12. A trader that chooses to be master a specific type of trading method or trading vehicles has a much better chance of success than the traders that just dabble in many different things and never make much progress.

13. A trader has to write a good trading plan while the market is closed to guide their trading while the market is open.
14. A trader has to manage their behaviour by acting consistently with their own rules.
15. "The answer to what's the trend? Is the question "What's your timeframe?" – Richard Weissman. All traders are simply trying to capture trends in their own time frame.
16. Set your stop losses far enough away from your entry point to avoid regular noise and fluctuations. Find your stop level first, and then position size accordingly.
17. The money I have made in the stock market was made through following the chart and the trend not from some prediction or opinion.
18. My biggest trading losses came from hoping, stubbornness, and bias.
19. My best trading has happened when I was the most open minded simply trying to answer the question: "What is the chart telling me to do now?"
20. If you have to ask others for their opinions about your trade you should not be trading you should still be in the process of study and writing your trading plan.

YOUR ROBUST METHOD

1. "Trade What's Happening…Not What You Think Is Gonna Happen." – Doug Gregory
2. Go long strength; sell weakness short in your time frame.
3. Find your edge over other traders.
4. Your trading system must be built on quantifiable facts not opinions.
5. Trade the chart not the news.
6. A robust trading system must either be designed to have a large winning percentage of trades or big wins and small losses.
7. The answer to the question, "What's the trend?" is the question, "What's your timeframe?" – Richard Weissman. Trade primarily in the direction that a market is trending in on your time frame until the end when it bends.
8. Only take real entries that have an edge, avoid being caught up in the meaningless noise.
9. Place your stop losses outside the range of noise so you are only stopped out when you are likely wrong.

New Trader vs. Rich Trader Thinking

Difference In Thinking

Beginner
Fears = Cut Winners
Hope = Keep Losers

Professional
Fear = Cut Losers
Hope= Keep Winners

YOU are the weakest link in your trading plan

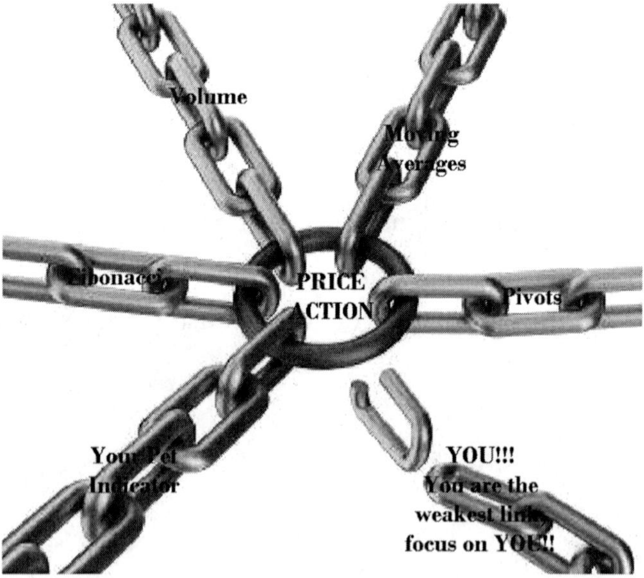

Words of wisdom from worthy individuals:

"I measure what's going on, and I adapt to it. I try to get my ego out of the way. The market is smarter than I am so I bend." – Martin Zweig

"To be a money master, you must first be a self-master" – J. P. Morgan

"Our greatest glory is not in never falling, but in rising every time we fall." – Confucius

"Buy that which is showing strength – sell that which is showing weakness." – Richard Rhodes

"The rule of survival is not to "buy low, sell high", but to "buy higher and sell higher." – Richard Rhodes

"Be patient. Once a trade is put on, allow it time to develop and give it time to create the profits you expected." – Richard Rhodes

"Be impatient. As always, small loses and quick losses are the best losses." – Richard Rhodes

"Never, ever under any condition, add to a losing trade, or "average" into a position." – Richard Rhodes

"When sharp losses in equity are experienced, take time off. The mind can play games with itself following sharp, quick losses." – Richard Rhodes

"When trading well, trade somewhat larger. Trade aggressively and trade larger." – Richard Rhodes

"Think like a guerrilla warrior. Fight alongside the winning forces. If neither side is winning, then we don't need to fight at all." – Richard Rhodes

"Markets form their tops in violence; markets form their lows in quiet conditions." – Richard Rhodes

"The final 10% of the time of a bull run will usually encompass 50% or more of the price movement." – Richard Rhodes

"My first rule is not to lose money. Losing an opportunity is minor in comparison, because there are always new opportunities around the corner." – Burt Dohmen

"Those who have knowledge don't predict, and those who predict do not have knowledge." – Lao Tzu

"Never hesitate to add shares in a stock that is moving higher but always avoid averaging down."

"Learn to take losses. The most important thing in making money is not letting your losses get out of hand." – Marty Schwartz

Amos Hostetter: Trading Don'ts

- Don't sacrifice your position for fluctuations.
- Don't expect the market to end in a blaze of glory. Look out for warnings.
- Don't expect the tape to be a lecturer. It's enough to see that something is wrong.
- Never try to sell at the top. It isn't wise. Sell after a reaction if there is no rally.
- Don't imagine that a market that has once sold at 150 must be cheap at 130.
- Don't buck the market trend.

- Don't look for the breaks. Look out for warnings.
- Don't try to make an average from a losing game.
- Never keep goods that show a loss, and sell those that show a profit. Get out with the least loss, and sit tight for greater profits.